The
Secrets
of the
Polar Regions

LIFE ON ICEBERGS AND GLACIERS AT THE POLES AND AROUND THE WORLD

ORIGINAL TEXT BY **BARBARA WILSON**

REVISED TEXT BY

VICKI LEÓN

LONDON TOWN PRESS

Jean-Michel Cousteau *presents*
Jean-Michel Cousteau
Publishing Director

Series Editor
Vicki León

The Secrets of the Polar Regions
Principal photographers:
Carrie Vonderhaar and Art Wolfe

Additional photographers:
Tom Bean/DRK Photo; Ralph A. Clevenger; Ken Cole/Animals Animals; Jeff Foott; John Fowler; François Gohier; Richard Hansen; Fred Hirschmann; Frans Lanting/Minden Pictures; Brian P. Lawler; Tom Mangelsen; Kevin Schafer; Twila Stofer; Tim Thompson; Larry Ulrich/DRK Photo; and Kennan Ward

Copyright © 2013 London Town Press

London Town Press
2026 Hilldale Drive
La Canada Flintridge, California 91011
www.LondonTownPress.com

Book design by Christy Hale
10 9 8 7 6 5 4 3 2

Printed in Singapore

Distributed by Publishers Group West / Perseus

Library of Congress Cataloging-in-Publication Data

Wilson, Barbara, 1949–
The secrets of the polar regions : icebergs and glaciers at the poles and around the world / original text by Barbara Wilson ; revised text by Vicki Leon.
p. cm. — (Jean-Michel Cousteau presents)
"Originally published as Icebergs and Glaciers: Life at the Frozen Edge by Blake Books, San Luis Obispo, CA, 1990."
Includes bibliographical references.
Summary: "Explains the creation, growth, and life of glaciers and icebergs with particular emphasis on the North and South Poles, focusing on the unique adaptations of plant and animal life living on or near the ice, in text and full color photographs" —Provided by publisher.
ISBN 978-0-9799759-0-5 (pbk. : alk. paper)
1. Icebergs—Juvenile literature. 2. Glaciers—Juvenile literature. 3. Ecology—Polar regions—Juvenile literature. 4. Natural history—Polar regions—Juvenile literature. I. León, Vicki. II. Wilson, Barbara, 1949– Icebergs and glaciers. III. Title.
GB2403.8.W55 2013
551.31'2—dc22
                    2008024732

FRONT COVER: Polar bears wander widely across Arctic regions of Canada, Russia, Greenland, Norway, and Alaska as they stalk seals. They live and hunt on sea ice, swimming from one floe to the next. As more Arctic ice melts, these vulnerable animals struggle to survive. Some bears actually drown, unable to swim across widening seas.

TITLE PAGE: The rubbery, round-headed beluga has a mobile mouth, which it uses to slurp up fish, mollusks, and octopuses. This whale makes a variety of sounds, from a chirp to a moo. Whalers of long ago nicknamed it the "sea canary."

BACK COVER: Walruses snuggle together to rest, sunbathe, and raise young. Global warming drastically hurts these ice dwellers. How? Females and young live year-round on ice sheets or floes. As ice melts, however, they're forced onto land, where hungry polar bears may attack—and panic causes larger walruses to trample smaller ones.

Contents

The icy reign of the polar kingdoms

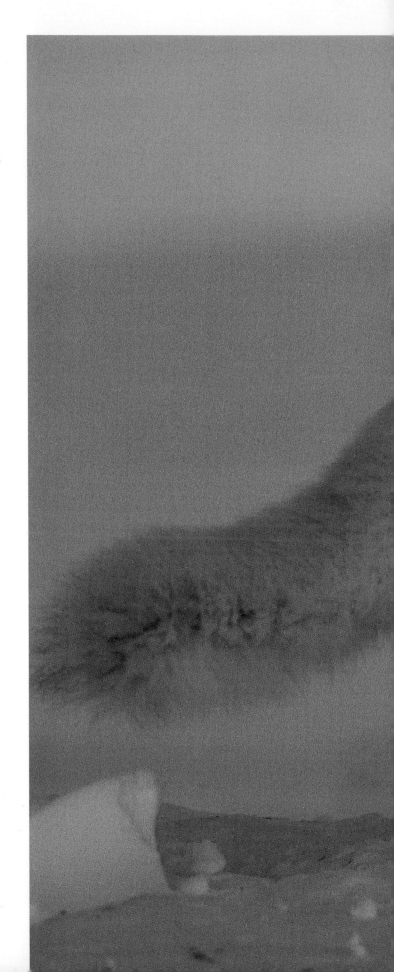

► In winter, the Arctic fox wears thick white fur to blend in while hunting snakes, hares, and lemmings. Heavily furred paws let it move well on ice. Since polar bears prefer to eat seal blubber, foxes follow them on the hunt to steal carcass leftovers.

Mention the North and South Poles, and we imagine the literal ends of the earth. Iceberg-rich, glacier-filled places where human beings are unwelcome and little exists besides bitter cold, howling winds, and months-long darkness. What we imagine is true. But there is also more beauty, mystery, and diversity in those remote polar regions than most of us ever dreamed.

From space, astronauts can see the Arctic polar region and its Antarctic twin. At that distance, they look delicate, decorating our radiant blue planet like vanilla frosting. In reality, these north and south polar kingdoms are vast.

The Arctic wilderness, much of it consisting of jumbled stretches of frozen ocean called pack ice, covers millions of square miles and extends across the top of our planet south onto the land edges of Asia, Europe, and North America. The geographic North Pole itself is located on pack ice, about three feet above sea level.

Hugging the opposite end of our planet is Antarctica, a continent twice as big as Australia, with mountains as high as 16,000 feet. Most of its land, however, is invisible, hidden by an ice sheet one to two miles thick. This ice sheet, a type of glacier, is made of fresh water in the form of snow that has fallen for thousands of years. The geographic South Pole sits on the ice sheet, 9,300 feet above sea level.

Both the Arctic and the Antarctic polar regions are complex ecosystems, a mix of land masses large and small, permanent fresh-water ice sheets, frozen seawater, and open ocean. They are dynamic systems, changing with the seasons.

It might surprise you to learn about the rich plant life and wildlife of these regions and their waters. At least 450 species of wildflowers bloom on the tundra lands around the Arctic circle in summer. The Antarctic has fewer plants on its land mass, mainly lichens and mosses.

Both places offer sanctuaries for a multitude of creatures to breed in safety: from seals and penguins to offshore whales and albatross. During summers at the poles, nearly non-stop daylight gives animal residents and visitors plenty of time to hunt, feed, mate, give birth, and put on weight to prepare for the bitter winter darkness to come.

In the seas around both poles, a rich food supply awaits. Hungry predators gorge on squid, shellfish, and a variety of fish species. Perhaps the most important food is krill, a plankton-nibbling crustacean that looks like a 2-inch cousin of the shrimp. It occurs in superswarms and is the main all-you-can-eat item for penguins, fur seals, fishes, and the baleen whales, including the blue, largest creature on our planet.

Plant and animal life also hide inside ice floes and on the undersides of pack ice in both the Arctic and the Antarctic. Scientists refer to icebergs as "floating islands of life," because of the quantity of organisms, large and small, that live inside, on, under, and around them. These include green algae called phytoplankton; the krill that feeds on such plants; the icefishes that feed on krill, and so on, up the food chain.

KEY DIFFERENCES: THE POLAR REGIONS

THE ARCTIC HAS:	THE ANTARCTIC HAS:
The North Pole, 3 feet above sea level	The South Pole, 9,300 feet above sea level
Floating pack ice, surrounded by land	Land covered with an ice sheet, surrounded by floating pack ice
Polar bears, walruses, beluga whales	Penguins, albatross, crabeater seals
Over 450 wildflower species	Mostly lichens and mosses
Average winter temperature (inland): -26°F	Average winter temperature (inland): -74°F
Midnight sun: June to September	Midnight sun: December to March
Human inhabitants	Human visitors (mainly scientists)
Aurora borealis	Aurora australis
Icebergs, glaciers, nunataks	Icebergs, glaciers, nunataks

◄ Adapting to its harsh environment, the polar bear wears layers of fat and fur insulation. It eats high-calorie blubber of seals to maintain its own fat reserves. Nevertheless, this bear is in real jeopardy. Scientists estimate that only 25,000 polar bears remain in the wild.

The two polar regions hold answers to many scientific questions about our planet. During the 1970s, in the skies over Antarctica, scientists were horrified to find that a colorless gas called ozone was disappearing. They already knew that ozone protects all living things on earth by absorbing harmful ultraviolet-B rays from the sunlight. Manmade spray cans turned out to be major culprits by using propellants of chlorine and bromine gases, which destroyed ozone and caused a depleted area popularly called "the hole in the ozone layer."

Working with scientists, world governments took relatively quick action. Such propellants were banned, which has kept a huge quantity of harmful gases out of the atmosphere. These efforts have kept Antarctica's ozone layer hole from expanding larger than it has.

Today the problems of climate change are even greater than the ozone dilemma. Time is running out. Can we save glaciers and the polar regions from the worst consequences of global warming? Some scientists still think so—and are working to do just that.

▲ Although native people in Canada, Siberia, and elsewhere continue to use traditional sled dogs, dwellings, and weapons, many of them have become dependent on the rest of the world's energy-wasteful methods of hunting, heating, and eating.

The top of the world

◄ Horned puffins rest on rocky cliffs during mating session but spend most of their lives at sea. They are terrific divers, swimmers, and fish catchers. Flight is another story. To get airborne, they often dive off cliffs or run along the surface of the water.

The word "Arctic" is Greek for bear. Long-ago astronomers gave that name to a constellation in the northern sky that looked like a bear to them. Later, the name came to be applied to the far north latitude line at 66.5 degrees, now called the Arctic circle.

The word Antarctic means "opposite the Arctic." It was coined many centuries later to refer to the southern polar lands, which the Greeks of 2000 years ago did not know about.

One summer around 320 B.C., a daring Greek explorer named Pytheas sailed north from Europe past Iceland, got to the edge of the Arctic ice, and saw an amazing sight: a land where apparently the sun did not sleep. People of his day scoffed and called his stories a pack of lies. Today we know that much of what Pytheas saw or guessed at was correct.

The variety of the Arctic wilderness is as amazing as its midnight sun. In some spots, the terrain rears up in rumpled glory, a blinding-white place where glaciers slowly grind valleys around mountains to dump their rubble into the sea. Arctic glaciers come in many sizes and types. So do ice formations, from gleaming see-through sculptures to small "bergie bits" that look like pieces of Styrofoam in the water.

The pack ice offers a stark contrast to mountains and glaciers, stretching for countless miles around the North Pole. Its varied formations puzzle our eyes. Some stretches are watery, polka-dotted with round ice floes. In other places, ocean currents cause pack ice traffic jams. Huge chunks collide, rearing up like giant ice cubes.

► The walrus stays warm, thanks to six inches of blubber. Stiff whiskers and long tusks help it find shellfish in shallow water. One walrus can gulp 3,000 clams a day! Since this pinniped eats and sleeps on ice, global warming puts it at risk.

How vast is the pack ice floating around the Arctic circle? Data from satellites show that Arctic pack ice in the winter covers over six million square miles. That is one and a half times the size of the United States. This ice has typically dwindled to three million square miles, or half its size, during summer. In the last few decades, however, summer pack ice has set new record lows. In the summer of 2012, for example, the Arctic sea ice covered just 1.32 million square miles.

Pack ice may look forbidding and empty of life. Nevertheless, a variety of animals live and hunt on it and below it, including polar bears, foxes, and walruses.

Despite their big tusks and bodies the size of Volkswagens, walruses are mild-mannered hulks that don't stalk anything much bigger than a clam. After rooting underwater for dinner, walruses spend their days in huge groups, sunbathing on ice floes. They aren't just relaxing. The sun's rays increase their blood circulation, turning the chubby animals pink.

Busier polar bears use the pack ice as moving sidewalks, jumping from floe to floe to patrol their immense territories and swimming miles at a time in icy seas. They hunt by stealth, using their keen noses and ears, lurking near airholes in the ice where a harp seal or a ringed seal will surface for its next breath. Although these bears may weigh half a ton, they are light as dancers on the ice. Their fur-lined paws give them extra traction to run at speeds up to 25 miles an hour.

Small Arctic foxes prey on seabirds, hares, and lemmings, but never turn down leftovers. They move with silent speed on the moving ice, often shadowing polar bears, on the prowl for seals. By hunting on ice,

Arctic foxes avoid competition from larger red foxes, who stick to land—and who sometimes snack on their smaller cousins.

Other mammals around the Arctic circle use glaciers as frozen freeways. Yaks, snow leopards, Tibetan antelopes, and ibex all migrate to their feeding grounds by taking the direct route over glacier-covered mountain passes. Come spring, the glacial habitat becomes an important feeding and breeding ground for a variety of species. Marmots and ground squirrels come out of hibernation. Ravens and snowy owls arrive to feed on lemmings. Other birds gorge on insects. Rosy finches and other species make their meals on the seeds—and occasional grasshoppers—that blow across the glaciers.

Smaller inhabitants of the Arctic also make good use of resources. One tough survivor is the glacier flea. Each night it freezes, hard as a popsicle, to the surface ice until warmer daytime temperatures free it. Then it wanders over the surface of its slippery world, searching for a meal of wind-blown pollen.

At the edge of the pack ice, lowlands called the tundra stretch southward, forming a bigger ring around the Arctic circle. The treeless tundra is as flat as fresh pizza dough. Most of the year, its snow-covered soil sits

► Camouflage, changing its fur from winter white to brown, helps the Arctic fox surprise its prey during the long daylight of summer. These small hunter-scavengers eat almost anything and can move on ice as well as tundra lands. It takes both parents to raise their litters of young foxes, called kits.

on top of a 1,500-foot layer of frozen ground called permafrost.

In summer, the surface snow melts, ponds form, and the soggy tundra shouts with color. Poppies, purple lupines, and cranberries race to bloom, while butterflies dance and blizzards of mosquitoes buzz through their brief lives.

Some residents turn color to blend in better. Foxes, weasels, and the Arctic lynx go from white to brown. Hares, a favorite prey animal, stay white year-round. Herds of migrating caribou (sometimes called

◄ The centerpiece of Denali National Park of Alaska is Mt. McKinley, North America's highest peak. This splendid region is still great country for traditional dogsledding.

Arctic deer or reindeer) graze the meadows, keeping an eye out for wolves—and for deadly wolverines. Brown bears and grizzlies prowl the tundra, munching mice and lemmings, sampling berries for dessert.

In parts of the North American tundra, moose lumber along, nibbling willows and wading in to eat underwater vegetation. At the same time in northern Europe and Asia, herds of musk oxen feed on tundra grasses and lichens. Despite their size, both moose and musk oxen must guard their young from sneak attacks by wolves and polar bears.

These mega-mammals get most of our attention. But inconspicuous plant species figure in the food chains of the polar regions, too. A one-celled alga has adapted to live in many ice-bound regions from the Alps to the Andes. Using a tiny beating thread called a flagellum to move, the alga gets into position below the snow's surface. There it spends its life, living on nutrients

▲ Husky musk oxen wear the longest locks in the animal kingdom. During summer, they shed one of their two fur overcoats. Sharp hooves let them dig through the ice for plants and climb rocky slopes. They roam the tundra, moving across countries linked by the Arctic Circle, such as Greenland, Siberia, and Norway. Although they often stand shoulder to shoulder to conserve energy and protect the young, musk oxen are fierce fighters and can give wolves a fatal goring.

dissolved in the snow. To filter harmful ultraviolet light from the sun, the alga produces pigments that tint its snowy home red, pink, or purple.

Other plants wait until a glacier retreats and there is enough nourishment to support growth. The thin soil left behind by glaciers is low in nitrogen, so pioneer plants tend to be puny and yellow in color. The cotton-like dryas plant is one of the first to appear. Later on, bigger vegetation from willows to spruce creeps closer. Once a glacier begins to retreat, it may take 200 years to build up enough soil for fir trees and heather meadows filled with colorful flowers to flourish.

Around the Arctic circle, even the skies glow with color, especially during autumn

▶ Dryas, sometimes called cotton grass, has white flowers that follow the sun, like solar panels do. This plant can thrive in soggy soil and is often the first to grow in an area after a glacier retreats.

and spring. The aurora borealis or northern lights draw curtains of violet, rose-red, and green in the heavens—a magical sight described over 2,400 years ago by that bold fellow, Pytheas the Greek. NASA satellites have now shown us that sunlight flows like a current through the earth's upper atmosphere. It causes intense magnetic storms, creating energy that we may see as shimmering colors.

▼ In places where glaciers have been, plant life gradually fills in. Stands of alder, hemlock, willow, and spruce trees take root and provide a habitat for bear, deer, and smaller animals. Ponds and lakes also form, such as this one called Blackwater Pond at Glacier Bay.

Imagine a nearly circular continent, surrounded by open seas that freeze into millions of miles of salty pack ice most of the year. Then try to imagine that continent frosted with heavy icing made of frozen fresh water, and you have Antarctica. Because its topping is miles thick, most of Antarctica has a flat sameness, with few landmarks to break the monotony.

The topping is actually a special glacier called an ice sheet. An ice sheet begins as a flat area or gentle slope covered with ice, fed entirely by snow falling directly on it. Because it rests on fairly level uplands, the ice typically spreads out in all directions. If the ice is thick enough, the pressure can even shove it up a mountain. The continent of Antarctica, with the South Pole near its center, is the ultimate ice sheet.

◄ The Weddell seal, a familiar sight around Antarctica, prefers to lie on snow or ice—and to give birth there. It spends winters below the ice, feeding on fish, squid, and crustaceans. This awesome diver can stay underwater up to 70 minutes.

► In Antarctica, the snow sometimes looks like someone has taken food coloring to it. Surprise: that tint comes from a living plant. In summer, tiny red algae plants take nutrients from snow and make a home. Red pigment protects the plant from the sun's harmful ultraviolet rays. There are over 700 species of algae on Antarctica—but only two flowering plants.

Tongues of ice, called outlet glaciers, sometimes escape from the main ice sheet. They depend on the ice sheet for nourishment, too.

Antarctica also has mountains, a few tall enough to poke through the miles-thick ice sheet. Such peaks are called nunataks and they occur in the Arctic also. They look like sharp islands of rock, sticking out of a white sea of ice and snow instead of water.

The Transantarctic, a 2,000-mile-long range visible here and there, divides the continent into east and west. Its most famous nunatak is the Vinson Massif, considered one of the world's Big Seven peaks. Another landmark is Mt. Erebus, the world's most southerly active volcano. This 12,444-foot peak always has a plume of vapor streaming from its crater.

Antarctica has only two flowering plant species—a pearlwort and a grass, both found on the skinny tail of the Antarctic Peninsula. But numerous other organisms, like lichens and mosses and hundreds of varieties of algae, eke out a living on rocks and meager patches of soil.

Arctic weather is challenging and cold— but the Antarctic climate takes the term "extreme weather" to a whole new level. The mean annual temperature at the South Pole is minus 58 degrees Fahrenheit but often dips much lower. Winds of near-hurricane force are frequent.

Very few creatures dare to spend the entire year on Antarctica. One is an insect the size of a rice grain called the Antarctic midge. Another is the sheathbill bird, an unpicky eater that gobbles everything from

dead fish to penguin poop to stay alive.

Unlike the frigid land, the nutrient-rich waters hold lots of life. Some species grow to gigantic size: the squid, the sea spider, and whales from sperm to blue whale. Other organisms like krill and microscopic plankton are small yet provide key nutrition to the giants—and others—in the food chain.

Most species, from birds to marine mammals, are part-timers. Periodically they swarm onto Antarctica's shores or use its waters and icebergs to breed, rest, or feed. They leave when the harshest weather sets in.

It takes amazing adaptations to survive Antarctic weather. Certain penguins can, thanks to special interlocking feathers. Each April, devoted Emperor penguin moms and dads trudge 60 miles through

utter blackness to reach breeding colonies on the pack ice. Once the female lays her 1-pound egg, she hands it off to her mate, who tucks it between stomach and feet to keep it warm. For two months, the males heroically huddle together, protecting eggs from freezing winds, while their half-starved mates hike back to the sea to fatten up on squid and fish. In July, female Emperors return to feed the new chicks, while the now-skinny dads head for the fishing grounds.

Two-foot-tall Adelie penguins, wearing their black-and-white feathers like tuxedos, spend winters on the pack ice, then march inland to find the same rocky sites each year to nest and raise chicks. Each Adelie tries to grab a nesting site in the center of the penguin rookery. Why?

Only two species of penguins call Antarctica home. One is the Emperor, a huge hardy bird with sleek movie-star looks. Adelies, pictured here, only weigh ten pounds but are just as tough. Other species live on islands near Antarctica. Why aren't there penguins at the North Pole as well? Because the Arctic is filled with ground predators— and flightless birds like penguins could never survive in such an ecosystem.

▲ Nearly the entire Antarctic continent is covered with a thick sheet of ice. From it, icebergs the size of a giant's building blocks drop their bulk in the sea. Winds and sea then sculpt the iceberg into fantastic forms, like this one.

Because hungry gulls and skua birds pick off many eggs and chicks from the nests around the rookery's edges.

Six other penguin species also breed and feed on the islands and in the waters around Antarctica, including gentoo, king, rockhopper, and chinstrap species. None of them can fly in the air. In icy water, however, penguins zip around like jets—and can soar out of the water to make spectacular belly landings.

Other seabirds fly the conventional way. Species from petrels to cormorants spend much of the year in Antarctica. They're drawn to its safe nesting sites and huge icebergs, handy as drying racks for wet wings. They also come for the abundant fish and other foods, including eggs and baby chicks stolen from penguins and other species.

The awesome albatross, the bird world's marathon traveler, nests on the continent and near it. It uses its wingspan of 8 to 11 feet to glide at high speed, up to 500 miles a day. All 24 species come ashore only to breed and raise chicks. Albatross twosomes mate for life, take turns finding food and feeding chicks, and think nothing of flying thousands of miles to do so.

Four kinds of seals live in Antarctic waters or on ice nearby. The crabeater, a misnamed pinniped that eats krill, not crab, is the most abundant seal on earth. Weddell seals spend the winter under the Antarctic ice sheet, using sound to catch prey and their buck teeth to nibble air holes in the ice above them. Competing for the title of most feared predator is the leopard seal, all gaping mouth and teeth. It hunts penguins, fish, and crabeater seals—but is often forced to fill up on krill. The Ross seal, rarely seen by human observers, prefers areas of heavy pack ice.

Female seals regularly birth their pups on icebergs or pack ice. This strategy isn't always successful. Killer whales, always on the lookout for a seal meal, sometimes bump new mothers, pups and all, off their bergs.

Antarctic wildlife is full of superlatives, like the southern species of elephant seal, the largest pinniped species in the world. An adult male may weigh five tons. Another interesting oddity are the fish families that have developed their own antifreeze to survive in these ice-laden waters. Some 120 species of icefish, plus an unrelated fish called the Arctic cod, have proteins in their blood that keep them from freezing.

The Antarctic skies put on glorious light shows that rival those of the Arctic Circle. Called aurora australis or southern lights, this breathtaking phenomenon is caused by the interplay between the sun's solar winds and the magnetic field of the earth.

It starts with snowflakes

◄ Mt. Kilimanjaro, highest peak in Africa, sits above the plain where zebra graze. The glaciers on its icy white dome, pictured here, have shrunk more than 80 percent; in a decade, they may be history.

For thousands of years, people have been curious about the early history of our planet and its icy regions. These mysteries remained largely uninvestigated until the mid-1800s, when scientist Louis Agassiz began to study glaciers in the alpine mountains of his native Switzerland. Even in areas without glaciers, he still saw many signs of glaciation. He began to theorize that our planet had seen many Ice Ages come and go.

Other discoveries confirmed his ideas. On other continents, North America for instance, he found more traces of ancient glaciers. The frigid island of Greenland, largely covered with an ice-sheet glacier, was still in the grip of an Ice Age. When explorers tackled the remote continent of Antarctica, they found an even vaster ice sheet. The Ice Ages idea turned from theory into fact.

Scientists today have studied ice core samples from many glaciers, some thousands of years old. From them, they've learned that the earth has seen numerous glacial advances and retreats. About 18,000 years ago, during the most recent advance, nearly one-third of the entire land mass of our planet was covered with an ice sheet up to two miles thick.

All over the world, clues from these long-ago glaciers still remain. There are mountains chewed into sharp peaks. There are valleys scooped out of bare rock. Still other hints come from gigantic boulders in places they do not belong.

Glaciers resemble slow-motion rivers. They are vast moving systems that accumulate snow and compress it into ice, which then wears away even the hardest stone.

A glacier is born high in a snowfield. In this accumulation zone, snow piles

► The Swiss Alps, where geologist Louis Agassiz made his important discoveries about Ice Ages and glaciation, are world-famous. Besides the Matterhorn, there are hundreds of other glacier-carved peaks, such as this one called Shilthorn.

up, winter after winter. Because the temperature stays low, the snow gets more compact. When it is more than a year old, the compacted snow is called firn, and its growing weight squeezes the air out of the snow layers. This action, combined with slow refreezing of water trickling from warmer surface snow, turns the firn into ice.

A glacier, however, is not just compacted snow that has turned to ice. If it were, anyone living in a northern city could study glaciers on city sidewalks. What makes a glacier different is its movement. When the compact snow and firn reach a critical depth, a glacier starts moving. Its bottom layer begins to flow like pancake batter. It slithers around obstacles, spilling downward, at first taking on the shape of the valley it is in.

As a glacier moves, it carries ice, picks up boulders, and drags along soil and chunks of surrounding terrain. Eventually, far down the valley, it deposits its load at its lower end. This point is called the tongue or the snout. At the tongue, the ice melts and drains off. Scientists refer to this place as the area of ablation or wearing away. Sometimes the rate of snow and ice accumulation is greater than the rate of ablation and we say that the glacier is advancing. When the wearing away is greater than the snow and ice fed into the upper end of the glacier, then the glacier is retreating or shrinking.

At its top end, a glacier looks relatively smooth and sleek. Further down, it gets bumpier. Although ice can stretch, it has its limits. Sometimes the surface of the glacier cracks, forming crevasses or holes more than 200 feet deep. In Antarctica, crevasses may be several miles long. Because fresh snow often hides them from view, travel is treacherous. People, dogsleds, and even large motorized ice vehicles can fall into these wedge-shaped pits.

As glaciers travel, they sometimes reach places where the underlying bedrock drops sharply. Instead of stopping, the glacier slowly "waterfalls" over a cliff, often making a crevass in the process. The most spectacular crevasses occur at the tongue of the glacier, where the oldest ice is.

▶ To understand how enormous the glaciers of Alaska are, look closely at this cruise ship in Glacier Bay National Park. The ship looks tiny but it holds thousands of passengers.

◄ From one helicopter, a photographer took this picture of another chopper. Can you spot it, looking like a mosquito against the gigantic blue-white cliff of ice? Below the tongue of the glacier, the surface looks like snowy ground. It's really open ocean, packed with so many icebergs of all sizes that it appears to be unbroken ground.

Glaciers aren't solid. Besides crevasses, they are filled with tunnels formed by meltwater. Many of these tunnels form mazes under the ice, making the interior of the glacier into a place of countless blue-violet caverns.

Geologists organize glaciers into categories. Alpine or valley glaciers, for instance, don't need constant nourishment from a snowfield. They begin in high mountains and are pushed down their troughs by snow avalanches. Cliff glaciers cling to small troughs on mountain faces. Piedmont glaciers fan out broad, flat masses of ice and are fed by higher-altitude glaciers.

Think about a glacier and you imagine awesome silence. Some make noise, however. As a tidal glacier gets near the sea, its tongue pushes ice into the water. This process, accompanied by huge rumbles and groans, is called calving. Instead of giving birth to a calf, the glacier produces a baby iceberg.

The offspring of glaciers come in different sizes—most of them big, bigger, and biggest.

Born in high snowfields, glaciers grow, travel, and sometimes give birth to icebergs. This feat, accompanied by rumbles and groans, is called calving. Most icebergs come from tidal glaciers like this one, the Grotto Glacier inside Wrangell-St. Elias National Park in Alaska. Although most tidal glaciers in North America are in retreat, some of those along the Alaskan coast, like this one, are advancing.

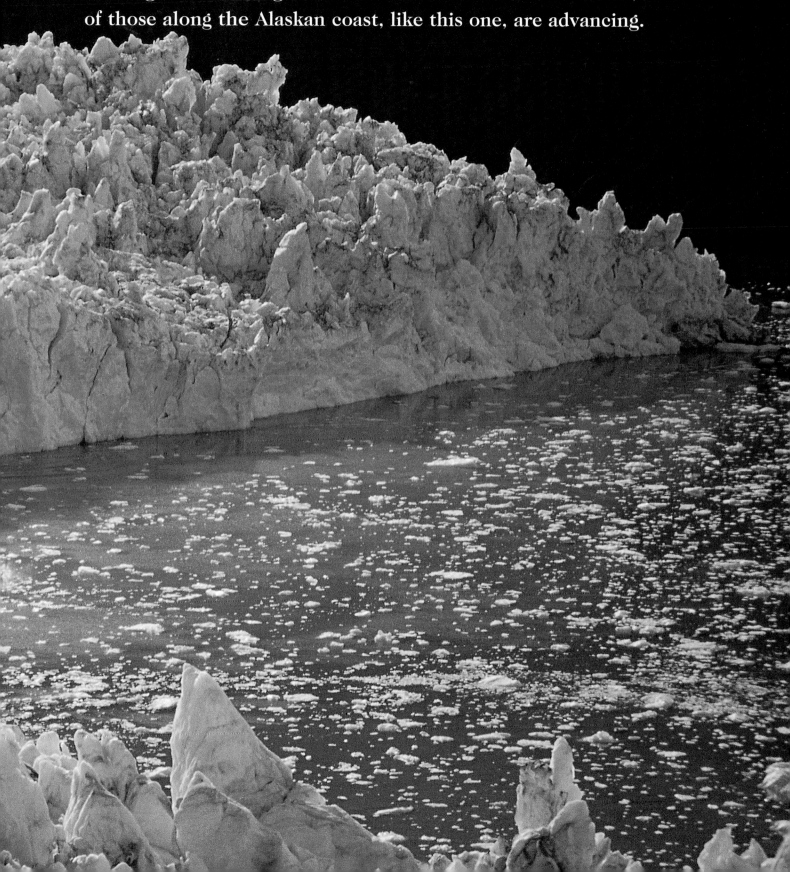

Most fresh-water icebergs seen in the Northern Hemisphere have broken off the Greenland ice cap, itself the size of Mexico. Some of these giants tower 300 feet above the sea. Greenland has also experienced glacier retreat and intense summer melting of its ice sheet in recent years.

Even bigger bergs break off the coastline of Antarctica, where thick plates of ice are fed by glaciers. In 2000, a monster berg called B-15 fell away from the Ross Ice Shelf. It was 170 miles long and 25 miles wide—about the size of Connecticut. Two years later, when the Rhode Island-sized Larsen B ice shelf collapsed, it shattered into thousands of icebergs. By one estimate, the amount released would have filled about 12 trillion bags with ice!

◄ Icebergs like this sparkling beauty sometimes get stranded on shorelines. According to experts, see-through ice is formed through pressure and may come from the the oldest layer in a glacier. When a stranded iceberg melts, it squeaks and burbles as air is released and the solid ice turns back into water.

---

big money on technology to help them spot icebergs in time.

Icebergs pose hazards to smaller vessels, too. Kayaks and canoes that get too close to calving glaciers or leaning icebergs may be swamped by the swells they cause.

Not all bergs are king-sized. Much smaller chunks of ice called growlers or bergie bits often litter the water near a tidal glacier. They too can be a menace to boat traffic because they often float unseen below the water's surface.

Unlike the ice cubes in our freezers, icebergs come in a variety of colors, shapes, and textures, depending on the type of ice that formed them and where on the glacier they have been.

Some bergs are gray-brown, pock-marked messes, loaded with sticks and dirt, the souvenirs of mountain peaks hundreds of miles away. Others made of denser ice are aqua blue. Still other icebergs have diamond fire. Their clarity and sparkle come from air bubbles trapped in their icy crystals, making them look like floating figurines or ice sculptures.

Thanks to their non-stop movements, glaciers have long acted as important

Large icebergs may wander for years, cruising through miles of ocean before melting. Four-fifths of an iceberg's height and seven-eighths of its mass lurk below the waterline. For this reason, they are a constant danger to ships. A giant berg blocking the shipping lane caused the Titanic ship disaster in 1912. Small wonder that many nations today spend

An ice cave gleams like a fantastical
jewel. It was probably formed when
meltwater streams at the surface of
a glacier tunneled their way into the
interior. Many glaciers are riddled
with ice caves but only a few, like this
one in Muir Glacier, can be glimpsed
by human beings.

◄ Explorers in the early 20th century endured much hardship to reach the North and South Poles and discover the wonders of the polar regions. Some of today's explorers seek adventure and overcome personal disabilities by challenging the outdoors, such as on the Ruth Glacier in Alaska's Denali National Park.

landscape architects of our planet. As a glacier rubs its thick icy body against its valley trough, it grinds away the bedrock. It tugs at rock fragments. It pries boulders loose. These movements make scratches, called striations, in the rock.

Geologists have discovered that glaciers carry boulders for long distances. The boulders act like slow-motion blenders, grinding some of the underlying rock into fine powder called rock flour. This powder gives glacial streams a milky color.

All of this slow, steady glacier grinding over thousands of years changes the shapes of valleys. What may have started as a V-shaped stream valley gets hollowed out, its sides scraped off, its walls pushed back as the frozen tongue of ice descends. Valleys shaped like Vs become U-shaped troughs.

In these valleys, high-altitude basins called cirques collect snow and hold it for centuries. At times, a big snowpack produces a cirque glacier, which starts moving backward, actually chiseling into its own mountain. When a couple of cirques carve away at one peak, their action leaves a rock ridge, as sharp and narrow as a knife blade, called an arete. Peaks sometimes get gnawed at on all sides by cirques, ultimately making a pattern of aretes called a horn. The most famous? The Swiss peak called the Matterhorn.

In their marathon wanderings, glaciers move huge amounts of material, sometimes dragging it hundreds of miles from its origins. At some point, though, a glacier lets its load fall.

The most curious objects left behind are gigantic boulders, some weighing over 100 tons. These boulders, called erratics, are different from nearby rocks. Due to their size and odd locations, erratics have inspired legends all over the world. Ancient peoples often used them to build religious and ceremonial structures. The Madison Boulder, one of the largest ever found, squats on New Hampshire soil, a rocky lump 75 feet long and as tall as a four-story apartment building.

Like earth-moving equipment, glaciers push piles of rubble and dump them elsewhere. Sometimes their action forms long ridges called moraines. Such moraines may contain sand, gravel, clay, and other elements quite different from the soil and rocks in the place they've been dumped. In other places, glaciers leave behind small hills called drumlins which can be 200 feet high. Bunker Hill in Boston is perched on such a drumlin.

Ancient glaciers have also spread quantities of a rocky soil mix called glacial till over much of the central United States and northern Europe. In places like Iowa, this material may lay in drifts 200 feet deep. Although it contains many rocks, glacial till makes excellent soil for farming.

At 2000 feet, it is easy to see how tidal glaciers flow to the sea, pushing their loads of rocky rubble as they go. Here, two mighty glaciers meet at Glacier Bay, one of Alaska's national parks.

The poles under siege

◄ Polar bears manage to survive in the harshest climate on earth. Unlike brown bears, their diet is limited to three species of seals. Their lifespan? Surprisingly short – 15 to 18 years. Their reproduction rate is one of the slowest among mammals. Polar bears give birth to twins or triplets that are blind, toothless, and completely dependent on mom for two years. But females cannot even have cubs unless they get enough fat to eat.

For thousands of years, the frigid and faraway ecosystems of the polar regions have remained pristine. The storms, ice, high winds, and low temperatures of Antarctica have discouraged permanent human settlements. The hardy native cultures around the Arctic circle traditionally used sustainable practices to hunt and fish.

Today, however, because of human population growth, exploitation of declining resources, pollution, and warming trends, both polar regions are in deep trouble. The Arctic is under particular stress. Snowfall is down, keeping ringed seals from making lairs for their pups. Winter sea ice, the platform of life for numerous creatures, is shrinking in size and thickness, hurting everything in the food web from walruses to polar bears to the tiny krill critters that live on strands of ice algae.

► Climate change has made the grizzly bear expand its range north, into polar bear country. Although the grizzly grazes on a varied diet of salmon, small mammals, berries, and bird eggs, it competes with polars over territory. This puts more pressure on the already endangered polar bear population.

Most scientists and world leaders agree that the magnificent ecosystems of our polar regions are in serious trouble. And glacial formations around the world are also sending us urgent messages.

Glacial ice has revealed ominous clues about our warming planet. Trapped in bubbles, scientists have located air, thousands of years old, containing much lower levels of carbon dioxide than ice today. Where do these skyrocketing levels of greenhouse gases come from? Largely from human populations burning fossil fuels.

The earth is also warming in another way. Pack ice (made of frozen salt-water and also known as sea ice) normally expands in fall and winter and shrinks in spring and summer. At its maximum extent, it covers nearly 13 percent of the earth's surface. In winter, the pack ice surrounding Antarctica covers six million square miles; the Arctic ice cap, about the same. This ice helps keep our planet cool by reflecting much of the sunlight that falls on it. These days, however, pack ice in summer, especially in the Arctic, is melting sooner, disappearing further, and getting thinner.

Climatologists also worry about the fresh-water ice sheets of Antarctica and Greenland. They contain more than 90 percent of the world's fresh water, although it is locked up as ice. The more it melts, the more sea levels will rise around the world, which could eventually drown coastal cities, swamp low-lying islands, and lead to inland flooding.

Most glaciers today are retreating. It's happening in China, in Canada, in Switzerland, in Africa, in Peru. Many are disappearing completely, some at speeds that have scientists and the general public very worried. Why the concern? Because meltwater from glaciers is the main source of clean drinking water for millions of people. As glaciers shrink, they no longer feed the rivers that people and animals depend on for water.

Another worldwide concern is the threat to wildlife. Top predators like polar bears are drowning or starving in growing numbers, unable to cope with the dwindling of pack ice on which they hunt for prey. Although tiny krill don't have as many admirers as polar bears, they are deeply affected by the loss of pack ice, too. Without the algae growing underneath the pack ice, krill have no food source. Scientists predict that global warming will bring on mass extinctions of numerous species—and in turn, famines for human populations.

The permafrost beneath the Arctic tundra presents another problem. Warmer temperatures cause it to thaw, turning habitat into mushy mire. As this happens, the land collapses and water-filled gullies riddle the ground. Melting permafrost also produces methane, another potent greenhouse gas.

They may be distant from population centers, but the polar regions are not safe from pollution. The growing human demand for mineral resources and protein from fish and whales, as well as carelessness and greed, have done significant damage. Oil spills have occurred in the Arctic and around the Antarctic. Both ecosystems have been polluted with plastic garbage, heavy metals, and other toxins. Such poisons are often found in the tissues of marine mammals and birds, a process known as bio-accumulation. Their immune systems weakened by pollution, animal populations fall prey to disease and decline more easily.

Although a few researchers still believe the earth is merely going through a normal cycle of cooling and warming, an overwhelming majority believe our predicament is manmade. Only with swift action, and a bit of luck, is it fixable. More than the polar regions are at stake here. The fate of fresh water supplies, of our lovely blue planet, and of all of us on it, hangs in the balance.

▼ The Mendenhall Glacier is steadily shrinking. Once near city limits, the glacier now sits 13 miles from downtown Juneau, Alaska's capital.

Secrets of life at the frozen edge

- Nothing goes to waste in the Antarctic—not even waste. Midges feed on penguin poop. So does the shearbill bird.

- Husky dogs are still used to travel around the Arctic circle. Not so at the South Pole, where huskies pulled dogsleds for a century before being replaced by motorized vehicles.

- Penguins look chubby but don't have much fat. Instead of keeping warm with blubber, as seals do, they stay cozy inside "wetsuits" made of special interlocking feathers.

- The world's largest critters eat nothing but some of the world's smallest critters. Blue whales visit Antarctica in summer, when the tiny algae called phyto plankton are at their peak and so are krill, the blue's main food item.

- Greenland isn't green. It's covered with an ice sheet three times bigger than all the glaciers in the European Alps.

- Polar weather isn't for sissies. Temperatures may reach 100 degrees below zero. Ground winds blow 200 miles per hour. And the non-stop daylight of summer is followed by months of total darkness.

- China's shrinking glaciers feed rivers that more than 200 million Chinese depend on for fresh water.

- "Bergie bits" break off glaciers and larger icebergs—but still may be the size of a house. Often bergie bits are deep blue. That happens to glacier ice when all the air has been forced out of it.

- Although its weather is brutal, Antarctica —and the small islands of South Orkney nearby—possess over 1,200 marine and land animal species, according to a recent comprehensive survey.

- Antarctica, home to the South Pole, is the coldest, windiest, highest, and driest continent on earth. It also has an active volcano that shoots lava bombs at times.

- As their habitat changes, some polar bears may adapt to the summer melting of pack ice by resting on large tabular icebergs that break off the ice sheet of Greenland. Whether they hang out on these icebergs or on dry land, bears find very little to eat or hunt. Why is that? Because seals, the primary food for polar bears, mainly hide under the pack ice.

- The storm petrel and the Arctic tern have the longest migration routes of any birds. Each year the petrel goes to the North Pole to feed, then to the South Pole to breed, a 25,000-mile round trip. The tern does just the opposite!

◄ The valley glaciers on Mt. Rainier near Seattle, Washington, are part of the Cascade Range and Rainier National Park. The Cascade glaciers, important as sources of fresh water, are retreating and losing mass faster all the time.

Glossary

Accumulation zone. The productive upper end of a glacier, where snow becomes compacted, forms ice, and then begins to move downward.

Aurora borealis, aurora australis. A dazzling light show that occurs seasonally in the evening skies, especially over the Arctic and the Antarctic. Scientists believe that solar winds, flowing through the upper atmosphere, cause magnetic storms that we see as shimmering colors.

Bergie bits. When icebergs break apart, the smaller pieces are called bergie bits. Often blue in color, the part of the bergie bit visible above water may vary from 12 to 75 feet.

Calving. When a tidal glacier nears the sea, its tongue pushes ice into the water, a process called calving. This is how many icebergs are formed.

Cirque glacier. This glacier begins from a snow-filled bowl on a mountainside. After snow is transformed to ice, the glacier gnaws into the rock. The Swiss Matterhorn is a good example of how cirque glaciers shape a mountain.

Climate change, also called global warming, describes the temperature increase we're experiencing on our planet. The U.S. Environmental Protection Agency says that global warming can occur from a variety of causes. Some are natural; others are caused by human beings, such as the growth of greenhouse gases. If we fail to control it, more extreme weather, natural disasters, and species extinction will likely result.

Growler. An iceberg type, smaller than bergie bits, and often clear. These two to 16-foot bergs are dangerous to ships because they are low, hard to spot, and unstable.

Iceberg. Icebergs can be made of fresh water or salt water. They often break off glaciers and float, sometimes for years, before melting. Some miles-long icebergs from Antarctica get as big as small countries.

Ice sheet. This type of fresh-water glacier takes thousands of years to form from fallen snow. It usually begins in a flat area and spreads out in all directions. Antarctica and Greenland are both covered with huge ice sheets.

Krill. Crustaceans that resemble shrimp. Krill move in superswarms and are abundant in the cold waters around Antarctica. Krill live on microscopic plankton. In turn, they serve as food for blue whales, fur seals, penguins, and certain kinds of fishes.

Latitude line. Horizontal lines, agreed upon by scientists and mapmakers, that circle our planet earth in parallel patterns. The latitude line of the equator divides the earth in two and is located at zero degrees. To the north, the latitude line at 66.5 degrees is called the Arctic circle.

Nunatak. Mountain peaks, found in the Arctic and especially the Antarctic. Nunataks are completely surrounded by ice sheets; only the sharp peaks poke through the thick ice and snow they sit in.

Ozone layer. The miles-thick layer of air above the earth that contains most of the ozone, a gas that protects living things from the most harmful solar rays. Human use of spray cans and other propellants has damaged the ozone layer; today the problem continues to be monitored.

Pack ice. Free-floating ice made of frozen salt water; also called sea ice. Around the North and South Poles, pack ice extends for millions of square miles. It grows and shrinks with the seasons and is not attached to land.

Permafrost. A layer of permanently frozen ground, two to 1,500 feet thick, lying beneath the active layer of snow-covered soil around the Arctic circle. Plants grow only in the active layer, which thaws for part of the year.

Tidal glacier. A glacier whose path leads directly to the sea.

Till. In places where a glacier moves over land, it drags and pushes soil and rocks with it. When the glacier retreats, it leaves behind a rocky mix of clay, sand, and other soil types called glacial till.

Tongue. Also called the snout, the tongue of a glacier is the leading edge and is made of the oldest ice. When it reaches the sea, the tongue pushes ice into the water, which forms floating icebergs.

◄ Beluga whales are dark gray at birth, gradually lightening to pure white or pale yellow by the time they are ten. Their strong tails help these orca-sized whales dive for squid and other small prey.

About the author

The original edition of Maryland poet and nonfiction writer Barbara Wilson's work appeared in 1995 under the title "Icebergs and Glaciers." This revised and expanded edition was written by series editor Vicki León.

Photographers

Major contributors to this book are:

- **Carrie Vonderhaar**, well known for her work for the Ocean Futures Society. Her photos appear on the front cover and on pp 1, 11, 13, 40-41, 46.
- **Art Wolfe**, internationally known for his striking animal portraits and natural landscapes. His photos are on pp 4-5, 14, 19, 20-21, 32-33, 38-39.

Other contributing photographers:
Tom Bean/DRK: pp 30-31, 34-35
Ralph Clevenger: pp 24, 44
Ken Cole/Animals Animals: p. 9
John Fowler: p. 36
Francois Gohier: p. 15, upper
Fred Hirschmann: pp 7, 27, 43
Frans Lanting/Minden Pictures: pp 16-17, 22
Brian P. Lawler: pp 25, 28-29
Tom Mangelsen: Back cover, p. 8
Tim Thompson: pp 12, 15, lower
Larry Ulrich/DRK: p. 47
Kennan Ward: pp 10, 42

Good websites & helping organizations

- Antarctica Project publishes wonderful resource lists for elementary through high school students. (www.asoc.org)
- Greenpeace fiercely spearheads the environmental defense of the Arctic and has a number of terrific YouTube films to watch and pass along. (www.greenpeace.org)
- Natural Resources Defense Council (NRDC). Besides their high-quality quarterly magazine, NRDC produces fact-filled bulletins at shorter intervals. (www.nrdc.org)
- Polar Bears International. A kid-friendly, well-organized website. (www.polarbearsinternational.org)
- National Geographic's website bubbles over with stunning photos and well-written articles on every aspect of global warming, from tundra to arctic critters. (www.nationalgeographic.org)
- The Arctic ice sheet, a true color map with daily updates in summer; fun to study any time of year. (http://www.arctic.io/satellite).
- The Nature Conservancy educates the public on climate change issues and in particular on the impact on animals such as polar bears. (www.nature.org)

► Not all of the water in a glacier is locked up as ice. Meltwater streams flow from some glaciers and at times become waterfalls. It can happen when a glacier leaves behind a hanging valley of rock, like this one in Yosemite National Park,

Books and DVDs, videos:

- *Frozen Planet: The Complete DVD and Blu-Ray Series* by BBC and David Attenborough (2012) and *Frozen Planet: A World Beyond Imagination*, companion hardcover to the series. From Antarctica's active volcanoes to the most remote parts of the Arctic: brilliant and comprehensive portrait of the world's polar regions. 3 discs.
- *The Mammoth Book of Antarctic Journeys* by Jon Lewis: 35 first-hand accounts of men and women who challenged the most daunting continent on earth. (Running Press 2012)
- *To the Arctic* by Florian Schultz, the companion hardcover to the IMAX film of the same name. (Mountaineers Books 2011)
- *Polar Obsession* by Paul Nicklen. The Arctic presented by a native photographer and naturalist. (Focal Point Press 2009)
- *The World of the Polar Bear* by Norbert Rosing. (Firefly Press 2010)

Valuable periodicals:

- *Onearth*, the quarterly magazine of The Natural Resources Defense Council (NRDC), is a superb reference and resource available to members but is also found in libraries across the country.
- *Sierra*, the bimonthly magazine from the Sierra Club national headquarters, is packed with useful and relevant articles. Sent to members but also available in libraries and at local chapters
- *Scientific American*, published monthly, is a challenging but deeply informative read, useful to teachers and librarians on hot-button topics such as climate change and animal science.

Index

Photographs are numbered in **boldface** and follow the print references after **PP** (photo page).